Mysteries of Light

Poems through a Prism

Rosy Cole

Copyright ©2021 *Rosy Cole*

www.pilgrimrose.com

The right of Rosy Cole to be identified as the Author of this Work has been asserted by her in accordance with the Copyright, Design and Patents Act 1988.

All rights reserved. No part of this book may be reproduced, stored in a retrieval system, or transmitted in any form or by any means without the prior written permission of the publisher or author, nor be otherwise circulated in any form of binding or cover other than that in which it is published and without a similar condition being imposed on the subsequent purchaser.

ISBN 978-1-7399801-0-8

New Eve Publishing

Great Britain

Light

Light

The visible reminder of Invisible Light.

T S Eliot

Four Wishes	10
Pearl Through Burnt Glass	12
The Fire Of The Frost	17
Eden Eclipsed	20
Reverie In Blue	23
Lord Nelson's Hat	25
Mirror Moon	27
Cutting The Diamond	28
Magdalene's Reflection	30
Dog Star	32
Harvest	34
Oh, Eve	35
Oh, Where Did Summer Go?	38
Mysteries Of Light	41
Where Bluebirds Fly?	42
Inside Out	44
Spell Check	47
What Winter Knows	49
A Mysterious Companion	51
Hide And Seek	57

Will You Dance With Me In Heaven?	59
I Hear The Music Now	61
The Ballad Of The Wild Sub-Rosa Rose	66
Between The Rainbow And The Dove	69
Judas' Lament	74
Vermeer's Muse	83
A Talent Set On Fire	85
Mirage	87
The Bridegroom's Song	89
Bread Of Heaven And Roses	91
Ruby Wedding	94
The Cello	95
Epiphany	96
Breakthrough	98
Uriel's Token	100

Four Wishes

...For time

to heal and feel and breathe
free air unlaced with taint of death,
to ponder skies of patent blue
and kindled clouds of sunset hue,
to savour moments where life lives
and know no situation gives
of itself and without cost,
for in pursuit true life is lost

...and space

beyond encroaching walls,
a banished need for shopping malls,
those boundaries of every kind,
breached on land, in heart and mind,
and false divisions that enlist
a pledge that puts us to the test,
removes our footprints with the tide
of crosshatched plots and national pride

...and place

where energies recharge,
a refuge from the world at large
so inspiration finds its wings,
hard-earned spoils each season brings,
where travel can reveal new cultures
but foils the money-changing vultures,
lends atmospheres that tell of history
and conjures legends wreathed in mystery

...and Grace

in time and space to find
a place within our heart and mind
of peace, emblem of that heavenly home
where pearls exchange for purchased loam,
furnished by One who pierced the gloom
and snapped the bondage of the tomb
and rose to greet a golden dawn,
a mystic presence in our form.

Pearl Through Burnt Glass

John Constable in Brighton

There is nothing here
for the painter
but the breakers
and sky
this place is a receptacle of fashion
off-scouring of London
Who am I in this
Piccadilly by the sea?

An August dawn
the tide
all mellifluous silk
and tattered lace
a reaper's sun
spilling carmine
along a linear horizon
shingle grates

underfoot
impedes motion
shifts and reforms
product of aeons
of attrition
and aggregation
a millstone
that belongs to no mill.

Maria, dear wife of my soul
mother of my children
who shunned an inheritance
to share my yoke
all but consumed
stumbles under the weight
of sheer mortality
tethered
tethered each
the seagulls circle and cry
and articulate
the presage of loneliness.

I want to tread no shores
I seek the inward path
through field and forest
the rugged ascent
that offers panorama
the cornfields
the sickle that gleans
the freighted haywain
the sky its own canvas
that chief organ of sentiment
I want mastery of colour
and chiaroscuro
the sound of water escaping
mill-dams, willows
old rotten planks
and brickwork.

I love such things...

I want to forget Ruysdael
and Rubens and Lorrain

nature depicted
sometimes wrested
to its own destruction
I yearn to render
the outer and inner
landscapes
perfectly matched
peopled mostly
the taming of wilderness
My pictures
will never be popular
for they have no handling
but I do not see handling
in Mother Nature.

I practise mood clouds
stride in safety
the chain pier
over a mercurial sea
I sculpt and limn fast
beachbound boats
anchors, creels

the real business of coast
light and shadow
never stand still
I collect red and yellow earth
to transport to my studio
and rake the walls of memory
for detail
while sunset fades
to pearl through burnt glass.

The Fire Of The Frost

'It is the life of the crystal, the architect of the flake, the fire of the frost, the soul of the sunbeam. This crisp winter air is full of it.'
John Burroughs, *Winter Sunshine*

A tribute to Scottish painter, Joseph Farquharson

I'm Laird of Finzean and the leeward hills
that hie from the skirling wind
on Aberdeen's shores
and heather-happed moors
my steads huddle close and kind

A refuge from alien thunder and smoke
away from the conflict and strife
the hell-smelling drifts
of death-dealing mists
the sore greeting of bagpipe and fife

Brave lads have gone out to rout the design
of marauders who scorn Scotland's past
its legends and lore
that swell the heart's core
with pride when they're called to *Stand Fast!*

Oh, joyless the blizzard that hones winter's blade
and wakes ghosts of the gone from their sleep
below leaden skies
despite the snow's rise
the shepherd keeps faith with the sheep

Unerring his eye when they wander the braes
and the blind bluffs and crags of the ben
his impatience he hides
and with helper he guides
his lambs to the lithe o' the glen

Untimely, my siblings are swallowed in earth
and the gloaming has doused mother's light
but we'll dance on the tartan
and make merry for certain

candles blazing to banish the night

For winter's the season that gave our bard birth
romancing the rose and love lost
and divine are the glints
that inspire rainbow hints
kindling the fire of the frost!

Eden Eclipsed

On the Feast of the Assumption of the Blessed Virgin Mary

I look for him the way he went
among the mists of dawn
when night gives birth to virgin light
and gilds the alien corn

I see him not and yet I know
he dwells within this sphere
His every gesture's melt and phrase
in others whispers here

We lost him once, in boyhood's rise
amid the journey's crowd
Our thoughts and wild assumptions
did heaven's vision cloud

So humbly did he bend his will

to exalt Cana's wine
A prompting Spirit turned his heart
and imaged the divine

I cannot tell, for words are vain
how absence fires strange joy
It burns away the wasting world
and strips the sly alloy

The light grows dim and human form
dwells in a shadow land
but yet its lucent nimbus tells
the Kingdom is at hand

And so I rise at dayspring's hint
and sift the shifting mists
for one familiar countenance
by realms of glory blessed

My feet imprint the Garden dew
loosen from earth's tether
Upborne on wings of bliss I pierce
the radiant ether

The flesh recedes, horizons clear
consume my being's see
Now is the time! My Love revealed
with arms stretched wide for me!

Reverie In Blue

Raw blue of paint on my first day in school
redolent of matches and crossed Union Jacks
raindrops, sunlit, clinging to the windows

Reckitt's Blue of rocks south of Windermere lake
rush of babbling cobalt from a factory sluice
rescued white linen on a Monday washday

Sapphire blue delphiniums in a neighbour's garden
sparkling blue of speedwell in strolled country lanes
spectral blue of woods in a burgeoning April

Cloth-of-Gold blue of a new school blazer
crescent mooned badge a bit like Byzantium
culled wisdom for life: 'Spes Mea Veritas'

Royal blue plaque for prize-winning gallery
azure organza of pretty bridesmaids' frocks
Alice blue congratulations, the birth of a son

Voyage blue of Quink in a newly-purchased bottle
vial of Bristol glass, perfumed with history
vault-of-heaven blue of Giotto in Padua

Mirage blue of the shimmering Mediterranean
fragile blue of rosemary, forking terracotta shards
Madonna blue of Renaissance, Infinity's embrace

Lapis lazuli beads and Mysteries of the Day
lagoon blue of Stanford's Bluebird, sleek sostenuto
limber blue of agapanthus above Funchal airport

Blue of conjunction with emerald and purple
blue of peacock and kingfisher, promising paradise
blue of twilight reflection, cooling the heat of day

Lord Nelson's Hat

Diamonds dazzle Lord Nelson's hat,
the vintage oak wind-sculpted on the hill
light-pierced from a bold, all-seeing sun
that nobly ponders summer's embers

Bronzed acorns slip their leather cups
reverberant upon the ground and proud
their forebears made those 'wooden walls'
on crescent tides that drove invaders back

Sheep browse a hoof-worn treadmill,
eschewing thorn and thistle where random seed
may take no root, no quarter gained by rising
verdure in the evening blaze of history's days

Wind burns its timeless song into the soul
Clouds flee to brood and congregate elsewhere
Earth braces for a remnant harvest home
Another spring, another life, another year...

But Michaelmas is bright with angel mist
the ether wired with energies of beating wings
The sun dilates its farewell *joie de vivre*, a whirling
cursor poised to link to otherworldly scenes...

Mirror Moon

Mystic moon,
riding voiles of dusk
earth hangs deathly still
in the glow of your
seed of honesty
you may calibrate years
in bakers' dozens
turning tides within
and oceans onshore
never begotten
though not for want of
moonshine and wishing

Mirror moon,
you hide the far side
while the world reflects
in your rear view glass
craving salvation
O moon, is it time?

Cutting The Diamond

'My crown is in my heart, not on my head; Not decked with diamonds and Indian stones...'
William Shakespeare – King Henry VI

She sits in splendour
but the throne's a lonely place
its crown freighted with
birthstones from no exchequer
symbolic, priceless

Merchants would trade them
for glittering pyrite dust
Monarchy's old hat
Judas' hand is in the dish
only lucre counts

The poor might be fed
the economy revived
the broken spirit

quantitatively eased within
such fools' paradise

Sacred endowment!
She tows our history's train
There is no telling
how this world's diadem's a
crown of pagan thorns

How are they to know
that blind obedience to
unifying grace
pulls torsion of the psyche
crucifies slumber

The ship of state rocks
but the figurehead and heart
defies detractors
and ignites what's best in us
Pure Diamond Joy!

Magdalene's Reflection

You see her in Renaissance mode
where prayer and sorrow meet
you see her tears like falling pearls
on his anointed feet

And there the marble vessel breaks
the priceless perfume's fee
gives scent of balm and burial
but, faith, she is not me!

For this repentant Eve is called
his mother's name like me
but I have hailed from Magdala
and she from Bethany

She took him to her hearth and home
ignored her sister's voice
who scolded her for indolence
while Jesus blessed her choice

He raised their brother from the grave
when heart and hope were gone
and by their willing trust revealed
how hidden glory shone

We'd sought the streets, the hills and vales
to find our souls' desire
the bridegroom who would stake True Love
no thought of Holy Fire

And what she learned, and what I learned
we shared in heaven's fold
that mercy cancels sacrifice
and turns our deeds to gold

As when beneath the blasted Tree
we wept at Mary's side
there sensed an echoed Gabriel
that Life and Love abide

Thus we three Marys helped him break
the coil of Satan's chains
two contrite Eves and One of Grace
saw Eden's gift regained

Dog Star

After Robert Browning

That's my last canine pictured on the wall
looking as if he were alive. I call
that piece no blunder, now.
A Canon Powershot and sleight of hand
captured his mischief and there he stands.
Do sit awhile and be amused.
I said this camera by design, for none
saw Maximilian - Max for short - composed
and would have missed him altogether,
his rump fast disappearing in the rearguard
of a hundred miles an hour tornado,
had it not been for A1 technology
and the patience of a saintly spouse.
Perhaps Di chanced to pat a seat and say
Come, sit with me on your part of the sofa
and harken while I spin tall tales of your begetting.
His tail would wag; he loved a tale,

the rhythm lulling silky, pendent ears,
adjusting the helter-skelter of his heart
to gentler pace, his dark eyes bright
with immemorial knowledge
of spells woven by camp fires at twilight,
the day's work ably done, aroma of rabbit
run to earth, now sweating in a stockpot,
pheasant plucked of feathers, fit for hanging.
(His, sadly, didn't work, so why should theirs?)
Max was of noble Spanish pedigree, she'd say,
his sire and dam a coupling from the gods,
embellishing her yarn with arcane words
like 'perambulation' and 'peregrination'
that rang vague bells, and words like 'stroll'
he knew had to do with new-mown grass.
He'd listen, rapt to be the epicentre of Creation.
There now, she'd croon. *Keep still. Good boy!* Click!
The flash would spark spontaneous momentum
and anguished squeals at apperception vanished,
nowhere the source of light found and rounded up.
But Good Boy meant rusks and rawhide treats
and that magic word which, once articulated,
bound the speaker on pain of mayhem: *Walkies!*

Harvest

When hope did wither on the vine
and cankered buds fell free
their blighted knots vouchsafed no gale
would rock the fruiting tree

And bring its sapid bundles down
their promise unfulfilled
their beads no golden solstice bless
nor vintage blood be spilled

No mangling winepress of the earth
would pulp the skin and flesh
nor crimson spirit swell the veins
with life and faith afresh

When hope did wither on the vine
it mocked the turning world
the oyster bore its grit in vain
no tears begot no pearl!

Oh, Eve

Oh Eve,
what did you do
when Adam rose
and gazed at you
the future bathed
in lustrous hue?

But how
to hold it fast
that moment pure
already past
serpent beguiled
the die was cast

Too late!
No use to cry
the milk is spilled
the honey dry
and fraught the bond
a ruptured tie

And Oh!
Where did joy go
and how retrieve
the garden's no
another chance
in bliss to sow?

Poor Eve,
he looked askance
when your desire
was for the dance
no melding but
dull happenstance

And now
you wander through
a world corrupt
a cheerless view
uncoupled, fumed
with taint of rue

Hope gone -

the demon's cue -
his figured hide
you wear in lieu
as if the snake
had swallowed you

Temptress,
the scorched earth's ruse
your smitten mouth
and bondage shoes
forsake! And die
or live to lose!

So Eve,
what will you do
unless accept
a Virgin True
who bore God's son
to start anew?

Oh, Where Did Summer Go?

I remember midsummer,
its suspended, airy plane
finding expression in lark song
and the low-toned reverie of bees,
the shadows shortest,
the gifting of reflected light upon light,
hazel-tanned skin, cool cotton frocks,
blowsy as dog roses spangling the hedgerows,
wild strawberries, clandestine orchids,
sweet nettles sucked of nectar,
the flick of buttercups against bare ankles,
meadows browsed by complaisant cows
whose ire was never piqued,
whose trust never seared,
by the odour of holocausts wafting
from the nearest steakhouse.

I remember teal-blue seas
in pearly flight, spellbound by mead moons,

breaking upon an amber strand,
clawing the glinting flint for purchase,
spume-flecking the air with crystal,
capricious and copious,
pebble-dashed and lost amid
ancestral memories of Nelson's Navy.
And Scottish burns that sang of heaven
and glimmered with carat gold,
molten strontium suns capsizing
over unfathomable lochs, the ideograms
of distant yachts etched upon them.
Magnetic June, baptising June, swift-drenching
earth and air through crackling volleys,
not dry-eyed, bootless, bellyaching, as now.

I remember the airy reprieve
of exams done, free-wheeling sport,
the sound of rebound against braced gut,
air-headed shuttlecocks pitched over walls,
kites resisting any contract with terra firma,
picnics in meadows without threat of trespass,
peaceful, supine, upon herb-scented grass,

puffball flotillas in the ether's ocean,
no fear of the vigilant eye of agri-business,
the barbed stiles, clamped wheels,
 padlocked gates and occluded pathways,
as if briar and bramble were not enough,
the fenced off game bred for bloodthirsty pleasure.
Once, the seasons formed a respectful queue.
Now, nature apes man and they are at war.
Oh, where did summer go?

Mysteries Of Light

The Rosary at the Birth of Spring

Primavera, first truth
year's born again baptism
heaven's windows wide, laundered light shedding
amnesty promised, earth's hallowed wedding
to a kingdom drawn close

Jordan's tainted river
now sanctified water
Cana's brackish springs become vintage wine
old wineskins rupture, proclaim the True Vine
our cup overflowing

Thus winter's defeated
and live current fêted
blood fired and rewired, streamed in the cycle
Communion Bread, a veiled miracle
revives spirit and soul

Where Bluebirds Fly?

They have cut down the trees
on which I hung my thoughts
for rearrangement
into coherent patterns

The branches were arteries
that turned my inspiration
into textured leaf
evergreen, sturdy, holm oaks

from the Mediterranean
whispering of sunflowers
rosemary, olives and lemons
in their natural element

sports ground of squirrels
schola cantorum of rooks
the wings of collared doves
sunspread upon the boughs

On windy days they rocked
with interior knowledge
of history and compound time
frail scions now remnants of hope

They have slaughtered my trees
in the full flush of being
for fear of litigation
and rumours of frenzied gales

Mammon destroys the planet
I said to the Lord. *Why must it?*
Behold the new perspective, he said
I am giving you the skies!

Inside Out

Modern translations of St Paul
said 'puzzling reflections'
in describing perception,
with a taunting, haunting interplay
of light and shadow, never the same
for two minutes together,
which made better sense to him
than the King James image.

To see 'through glass, darkly'
was like tilting with a shroud
You couldn't tell what was on the other side
of cloak and gesture,
whose storyline it was,
and whose the wider plot, when to engage
and how to abstract meaning
from a colloquy already begun.

He liked landscape art
shimmering through a summer haze,

nothing clearly defined, merely suggested,
sketched and stippled
Precision was death,
the vanity of nailing flesh to a cross,
hoping the spirit would not escape
to recite its lore elsewhere.

Whereas hyperrealism, all die-hard hues,
stirred menace by osmosis,
Magritte, Chagall, Picasso, hit the spot,
dredging themes and schemes
from where it mattered most
Those artists knew a thing or two
about immanence, hypnagogic dreams
and shapeshifting metaphor.

Such designs granted form to feeling,
which delivered its own relief
without any rationale, the need to decode,
or the knife-twisting alarm
at having been jumped from behind
into action that didn't fit the fable
Hamlet and Hedda Gabler a Disney parody,
the diapason trashed.

Putting a foot in the wrong camp
was a hazard of moving and breathing
There was seldom signage to say where you were,
no cue as to what came next
in the pantomime of human exchange.
You had to hang around
until the swirling atmospheres composed a vision
you knew meant business.

One dusk, passing the Stage Door,
he turned into the Square to confront
a revelation of community. There, in the foyer,
under constellations of lamps,
theatre-goers were sipping and laughing
and gesticulating behind glass,
no script, no hard and fast plot; the miracle
of doors parting on proximity.

Next thing he knew was a stifling warmth
and billows of babbling energy
He'd thought to be among long-lost friends,
in focus, the jester at the party,
but the baffling palaver made him feel like a spectre,
an outsider on the inside,
so that he fled into night's embrace,
all lacerating noise and winking alarms.

Spell Check

You don't need spell check
to know Love's
a four-letter word

linguists can't argue
lovers might
the metaphor's tame

but nowhere near tamed
no science
just subtle aspects

of configured stars
synergy
of latent forces

neither is the blunt
archaic
word synonymous

Love's neither shorthand
nor icon
nor tailored to fit

tethered and tagged, you
can't save Love,
upload it to Cloud

it plucks the moment's
ripe apple
and plants next year's crop

prodigal spirit,
for some that
goes without saying

others sustain the
deficit
with coin of far realms

What Winter Knows

Triumph of morning
clear as a dazzling mirror
banishing hoar-frost
splintering ice over ruts
releasing trapped air

fretted oaks moss-lit
engross a blank horizon
synapses inert
like old folk at the bus-stop
waiting for a ride

ammoniac wind
scours the sinuses
of forsaken woods
June a mulch of memories
restoring root sap

skeletal boughs
stitch oblique shadows
to the westward fields
widgeon surf silver air
chevron-winged and sure

Hope tunes the theme
stirs buried longing
sunrise breaks upon
enamelled blue skies
O wonder! O Oriens!

A Mysterious Companion

We had hung around
those who followed him,
on the fringes
of what was going on
Something about him
magnetised us -
a harnessed energy -
His actions were natural
as running water,
performed with gentle
economy of movement,
as if integrity
on every front
was key to healing
and wisdom's pearls
must not fall foul
beneath forked feet
His words singed
a place in the memory

for Good, echoing
of a past and future Now,
strange cadences
on the tongue
of a Nazarene.

The women held their breath,
rapt at the sight.
Adam was in focus
and the locus
of their response,
the chambers of the heart.

He drew the children
with no sweet enchantment,
no narcissistic guile,
only the gift
of their reflected selves
within God's eye.

Next thing we knew,
they'd laid a charge

of gross profanity
against him
He was the pinnacle
of innocence to us.

They slaughtered him
to feed carnivorous appetite,
an orgiastic rite
Pitch night
eclipsed the light
and Jerusalem was mute.

Turning tail, we trudged
the homeward dust
we'd shaken off
without a second thought,
retreating to a shell
that did not beckon
and reckoned with
no warmth and welcome
Where were we headed
but to an emptiness

we'd gladly forsaken?
We knew well enough,
as twilight empurpled
the day with regal shades,
imparting mystery
to our deadened tones,
that something momentous
had taken place
We could not match
the expectation
still suspended in the soul
with unrewarded dreams
We seemed no longer
enough for one another.

When all at once,
our quantum leap of longing
begat a perfect stranger!
Unaware of the demise
of Israel's hope,
he kindled a flame
so bursting bright,

it cast new light
upon unfolding history
and pulsating promises
of scripture
We didn't want to part
and begged him tarry
at our door, come,
cross the threshold,
illumine our gloom,
set our hearth ablaze,
share our supper,
drink our wine,
let not this day's vision
go stale on us!
Our yen to seal the bond
compelled oblivion
of the meagre larder.

The tactile planes
of earth dissolved
into heaven's board
and victuals spread

before our Guest,
he blessed,
and broke the bread -
such precious fare
within his hands -
as if he would return our gift
with value manifold
How blind! How blind
our flesh and blood!
We knew him then,
our Host!
That instant, he was gone...
bequeathing us the Holy Ghost
Had we prefigured him,
or he us?
In consuming,
he was himself
consumed
and by that means,
he made us Whole.

Hide And Seek

Why do the charmed play hide and seek
and flee the story in the wings,
as if disporting on the stage
could set alight the curtain fringe?

Illusion's limelight's highly prized
and channelled sentiment extolled
If structured context cramps the style,
another's script makes players bold

The play's the thing, so says the Bard,
our psyche's lineaments laid bare
We revel in the story told
and all vicarious life is there

The Safety Curtain functions well
as acts meet their appointed ends
Perplexing shadows haunt the wings
Beyond, the brave face skylit lands

So who'll forsake bewitching masks
and don his natural God-given role
and tread the existential boards
and free the glittering eyelets' soul?

Will You Dance With Me In Heaven?

Will you dance with me in Heaven
where no earthly lines are drawn
Will there be a grand renaissance
of the time when we were born
into an age that's long bygone
with eloquence unspoken
Shall we step in time
in Heaven's Holy Joy?

Will you sing with me in Heaven
of that bright Ascension Day
when an evening celebration
shot with jewelled rays of May
saw glances fuse, invoke the muse
with chords of recognition
Shall we harmonise
in Heaven's Holy Joy?

Will you stroll with me in Heaven
through the soft and tender green
under skies of compassed blessing
lighting evidence not seen

in the former dispensation
of a Grace confined but true
Shall we walk on air
in Heaven's Holy Joy?

Will you praise with me in Heaven
Shall we join the angel throng
paying homage to the Saviour
in the place where we belong?
With the pilgrim journey ended
and the vision sought and found
We shall glorify
In Heaven's Holy Joy!

I Hear The Music Now

'There is meaning in every journey that is unknown to the traveller.'
Dietrich Bonhoeffer

I am breaking in two
Hell opens its mouth wide
bidding Heaven fill it

Am I a whited sepulchre?
pacific as Christ
before my warder
when a heart of anger
rages under the ribs
at living blasphemy?

Pictures from the past
assail the mind
taunting and tantalising
a Beethoven sonata at dusk

my fingers dabbling harmonies
from liquid keys

preternatural chords
that could transform
a disordered world

Vintage values, vintage leather
a timeworn oaken table
rye bread, sauerkraut, schnitzel
blessed conversation
the family as one dipping
its hand into the dish

My sister's merriment,
her sparkling wit, she with whom
I shared a sacred womb

Tubingen, the Neckar's sheen
willow-teased and placid
ancient gables pinked against sky
the halls of learning

*prescriptive ink, mottled parchment
a smell of dust and destiny*

*Embattled senses piqued
drunk on heroic visions
Wagner, Schiller, Goethe -
donning the mental shoes
of Luther, Hegel, Kepler
confabulating new fire*

*The zeal of youth!
The rampant certainty
good systems of belief
might slay hubris and heresy
Christians foiled, resisted, banned
the torque tightening*

*But no cheap Grace,
Grace the other side of pain
and prayer, Grace prodigal
and purposeful, power-releasing
stone-breaking Grace*

of Heaven's radiant geode!

Orgies of cleansing
God's Chosen hounded, trampled
the burning and the broken glass
the Prince of Darkness
determined to exterminate
his own reflection

The hiding, oh, the hiding
hand-shielded whispers
earthquaking jackboots
persecution by a buckled cross
the leading where I had no wish to go
like the Lord's disciple

I ask the warden how
his feverish daughter does
footsteps clatter in concrete corridors
echoing against the mindless walls
It is Time, O Lord. I am Thine,
You bid me come and die

O perfect irony! O Spring!
A round, rose-tinted dawn!
Birds fly upward like broadcast seed
I see the outlined noose, the narrow way
the gallows way, a doorway framing light
This, this is where it begins...

I hear the music now...

The Ballad of The Wild Sub-Rosa Rose

He plucked a wild sub-rosa rose upon the mountainside
Where gentian and edelweiss waved in the flowery tide
He gave it to the maiden who accepted it, bemused
't was not legal tender, but he could not stand accused

No courtliness his form expressed; it seemed he made for sport
To play the game with levity a well-bred maiden ought
The stolen bloom was currency in realms of make-believe
Feigned heart and soul of romance made for sniggers up his sleeve

Glib ardour did not move her, yet his perseverance did
He'd watched and learned to walk in step; how could she then forbid
So serendipitous a tie upon the outward path?
With no comparison to hand, 'twas easy on her faith

The peaks shone white as angel robes and crystals flecked their folds
Their treacherous crevasses hid beneath the frigid cold
The pair had chanced it merely to the halfway point by train
Where summer meadows capered in the gentle warmth and rain

He told her of a palace carved in ice upon the crown
A crossover on skaters' blades defence for fragile bone
The air was thin as razors, only ravens soared the clouds
He hinted not at windows showing lachrymosal shrouds

Some day they'd venture upwards and skim the glistening planes
Glissando was his forte; a Pied Piper's fluting strains
She heard, and wondered wistfully at such a scheme of things
Enough his love for two, he said (his gift for wind and strings!)

On Valentine's Day evening, he pitched her a proposal
The moon rode high in vap'rous air, prospecting betrothal
I think you've jumped the gun, she said. I know, he said, it's true
A salvo on still waters can do much to shape the view

They married on a luckless day of obfuscating mist
He, confident that wedlock would add substance to dull tryst
Bade welcome from his balcony, benevolence well-mocked
She tried to cross the threshold, but found the door was locked

Years passed: the wild sub-rosa rose had withered on its stem
She'd placed it in a casket and lamented 'twas no gem
Those blood-black brittle petals told a truth beyond its thorn
There's no buried cache of pearls when an errant knight pours scorn

On the heart and soul of romance in favour of brass tacks
Oh, ash before the embers! And no plaster for the cracks!
A castle on false premises is a parody of wealth
With dazzling manifesto, he captured her by stealth

Lo! the cockles of his heart are hollow as bare graves
Material expense can't buy the character he craves
The walking dead reaps debt, to neither flesh nor soul gives host
His alibi for living, a smoke and mirrors ghost

For he was never honest and elusiveness cost dear
He concealed so very smartly a taste for him, *not her*
What matter if clandestinely he donned a different head?
To betray her with her gender was running in the red

So the flower proved a symbol of travesties untold
No blissful bee alighted on its pollen-pad of gold
When the fateful dart struck home, she determined to be free
And burned the wild sub-rosa rose for all eternity!

Between The Rainbow and The Dove

On the Feast of The Transfiguration

We followed him through the foothills of Tabor
leaving the world's clamour behind
sounds muzzled by distance and heat-haze
and the remoteness
of another sphere
the sardonic scree irking our toes
but we climbed
dauntless as mountain goats
glad of the umbrous oaks and green-beaded olives
offering a truce between Heaven and Earth.

The hillsides glowed pink with rock-rose
the yesterday, today and tomorrow plant
that spends its petals prodigally
and births new buds
with glad abandon
Our feet clove galaxies of groundsel

the glory of Joppa
like miniature suns
while bees gleaned pollen from the Nazareth iris
and the white-bosomed dove marked our progress.

All about us, the hum of millennia
a tranquillity not to be found on rooftops
It seemed to embody history, but renounce it
the clanging cymbal of Rome
the clumsy fist of Herod
dispersed to dust and dereliction
and we catchers of fish
and fishers of men
on the dynamic threshold of a new order
might expect the desert to blossom as the rose.

I wished Andrew could have been with us
Our meagre catches lately weighed him down
He was cumbered with holes in the network
and daily bread wasted
not cast upon water
The family needs sustenance, he said

Caring for others
he understands that
We left him working fingers to the bone
fully equipped for when the tilapia rose.

Once, I took a coin from a fish's mouth
Whose head does it bear? the Lord asked
Why, the Emperor's, I said. Whose else?
Then yield him in kind
and accord God the rest
You'll have treasure in Heaven
The memory smote
linked to my brother
for that day he chose the way of mammon
and marred faith's vision.

We lingered to drink at a waterspout
Rock overshadowed us like shelter
The scene fell under the Lord's surveying eye
his brow brooding
his heart leaden
Down there, he said, in a cloudburst

did Barak defeat Sisera
the Canaanite chariots
grounded and confounded by God's hand
Deborah's faith molten in song

Time's steed was bridled for one split second
The hoarse roar of the embattled
assailed us, the collision of star-crossed steel
weapons washed in blood
terror-stricken mounts
bone architecture smashed and vitals pierced
God's hand sustaining
but not ordaining
Psalms of promise trampled in conceit
the price of shadows lent form.

We saw his harrowing, the sun half-hid
as if he gathered what was to come
The dove crooned its lullaby lament
The fountain quivered
A rainbow shivered
and rendered him in gold inenarrable

discrete and in relief
Oh, such relief
as transported us to where no pain was!
Glimpse of our uncharted journey's end.

Judas' Lament

Since Eden,
the serpent in the garden
and occult worm coiled in the fruit's core
have been troublesome.

That day,
his shadow fell across the door,
the man with the softly penetrating gaze.
The warped timbers stood ajar
so that the shrunken laths,
hanging on rust-mottled hinges,
allowed a shard of sunlight
to search out the dust and debris,
long accumulated
for lack of husbandry.

Some kind of god, he was,
strolling the seashore,

more Greek than Jew,
the structure of his very bones
a numinous amalgam
of meekness and confident authority.
The rugged, bronze-limbed fishermen,
uncouth and ignorant,
were drawn to him as to a magnet-
and he to them -
tax-gatherers and tavern-keepers,
whores and dice-casters in shaded alleys,
women haggling in the marketplace,
ragamuffins playing tag about the stalls,
the myopic Scribe who could not see beyond,
all flocked to hear him, spellbound,
as though he were some Attic orator.
He was the friend of everyone
but the Establishment
whom he confounded.

I wanted anarchy,
a new aristocracy.
I was a Judaean, for heaven's sake,

not a coarse Galilean like the rest of them.
If he really was our Messiah,
I wanted 'in', to be an insider
at this outsider's bolt from the blue,
part of the ensorcellment.
I wanted his bearings, his eloquence,
I wanted to be him!

Later, the day he passed the door,
he caught me in the Temple courtyard,
his anger blazing at wheeler-dealing
in the name of neither God nor Roman.
Oh, he was a glorious firebrand,
tipping over all the tables,
the coins jingling and rolling in pigeon-dung
like Satan's chaotic lottery!
I stood on the sidelines, watching,
neither for nor against such commerce,
and he fixed my eye with his own
and drowned me
in such pain and tenderness
that I was recalled

to our first encounter.
'Will you follow me, Judas?' he asked.
'Will you make up the dozen?'
'Lord, by my calculation that makes thirteen,
but I'm not one to scruple!'
'Then one of us is in error,' he replied.
'But come. Do not tarry longer.'
So I gained an entrée to the tribe,
recalling from his Parables
that dividends were the same for latecomers
as for early uptake.
No stranger to the tally,
my acumen was primed
to keep the privy purse.
A good steward, I'd heard him say.
The New Kingdom
could have no foundation
on poor investment of talents.

There was no doubting
his charisma, his way with words,
the pacific aura that seemed at times

to hold the corners of the universe.
They said he could command the elements -
such marvels and miracles!
But what was that to me?
My debts
weighed in the balance
just the same.
Ask, Seek, Knock, he said.
It made no difference.
I saw the evidence of change in others
but the door opened not to me.

He mirrored
what I should become
and mocked
by the comparison.

It came to a head when we dined at Bethany
where he'd exorcised the death of Lazarus.
Mary, a scandalous woman,
made an extravagant show of thanking him.
They were paupers, that family.

How came she by the jar of spikenard
she broke so wantonly over his feet,
filling the house with the stink of it?
(Let's assume it was purely gifted to her.)
Weeping, she soothed in the fine emollient
with wild, dark rivulets of hair.
It stuck in my craw to watch.

Surely, if he had been God's son,
he would have known
what manner of female she was.
'If her soul be true,' I said,
'shouldn't she have sold this flask
and given the proceeds to the poor?'

The nudge did not move him.
Within the pulled shadows of the oil-lamp,
he made some mystic comment
about her motive and the day of his burial.
It seemed he knew he was done for.
The Sanhedrin had him down for a blasphemer
and needed only a cue to arrest him

under cover of darkness

My heart sank.

For all his gut-churning appeal,

I'd backed another loser in the game of life.

He was a genius of sorts,

the Kingdom a mere projection of himself,

a good fantasy; inspiring, harmless.

It had no teeth

and would vanish like vapour at dawn.

Messiah? The notion kindled a burning pathos.

We were all in the grip of it,

sold down the river.

How I wished it could have been otherwise!

From there it was downhill,

from bad to worse.

I felt in my marrow the enemy closing in.

If he were captured,

how should we be free?

Safer to side with the Establishment now!

Perhaps he deserved the benefit of the doubt,

but I had neither the fibre nor will.

He knew that one of us
was drawing falsely on his account.
We reached to dip our bread together in the dish
and he looked me in the eye as he'd done
that first day, with piercing sorrow
and a strange vibrant resolution
that crystallised mine.
'Do what you have to do,' he said,
'and do it quickly.'
I felt a great fish turn tail in the waters within.
He was giving me permission to be myself!
Whether traitor or patriot, I knew not,
only that his moonshine wasn't for me.
Without a glance at the others, I left
and reported to Caiaphas that, by and by,
the wanted man should be found in the Garden.
My kiss would distinguish him.
My farewell kiss.
Stranger, I kissed him into Eternity!
I did that!

Thirty silver shekels they gave me,

the sum due to his master for a slave
accidentally slain.
And now I know, I know the truth
and it is too late, too late...
I grope the black abyss
and my innards are in torsion,
biting the purchased dust.

You see, I wanted to be him.
But he wanted to be *me!*

Vermeer's Muse

I am passing through
a sequence of spun still frames
shedding, showering
rhythmically recycled
ephemeral dust

This too solid flesh
belongs to time's illusion
I am a whisper
in your head, a quickening
of the soul's marrow

I am mere cipher
reflection of perception
I, a backward glance
down the halls of memory
glimpse of future past

Yet am I present

in the consummate design
unpolished carbon
scintillating in the beam
of a loving eye

I am passing through
one, two, three, four dimensions
God exquisitely
aligns the daguerreotype
eternal lustre!

A Talent Set On Fire

'Genius is talent set on fire by courage.'
Henry Van Dyke

Genius is interior light
the fathomless world of the crystal
caught in a needling sunbeam
or quivering candle flame

It is not of itself intellectual
nor inspiration, acumen, slick memory
the crisp organisation of words
on the uninformed page

Genius burns without consuming
like Moses' bush on Sinai
discard your mental shoes
this is Holy Ground
a penetrating glimpse
of form and meaning

hard edges melting
in luminous mist
patterns within patterns
reverberant echoes
from wild forgotten caves
pounded by tides subject
to lunar magnetism
the synaptic lightning
forked from the lodestone
of archaic memory

The landscape of genius
is the sheer rock face
grappled with irons and grit
for a squint at Eternity

Mirage

In aerial latitudes
and the silent margins
of heat and cold,
day and clairvoyant dusk,
the mirage shimmers
above our wilderness,
evoking plangent echoes
of something lost and longed for...

Risk the serpentine defiles,
the jackal's jaws and searing sand,
risk the rugged rocks for miles
to gain a purchase on the land
rendered in such high relief
There we shall slake our dusty frame!
The image pales and comes to grief
All and nothing is the same.

So where to turn and how contrive
the lineaments of real estate?

To dream, to sow, to dig, to strive,
to build, to spend, to save, to wait,
though noble empires wax and wane,
high thought and politics our pitch
An out-of-line design's our bane
Exchequers fail to make us rich.

A siren is illusion's muse,
her laurels bringing frail content
Ironic humour bucks the ruse,
the stage, the screen, the game, were sent
to occupy the vision's see
If only this, if only that,
had shaped our path, we should be free
by now to revel in delight.

The mind's eye is the heart's big screen
beguiling fictions into facts
Daydreams breathe lustre on the scene
Our footprints follow in those tracks
Away the promised land foursquare
whose substance sinks in shadow's maw!
But, mind! The mirage memory
reflects a true celestial shore!

The Bridegroom's Song

A poem for Advent and Pentecost

I see her coming through the mist,
my bride, my longed-for bride,
by showers of golden spent leaves kissed
and dreaming of my side.

The blood-pooled byways haunt her gait
False echoes drown the true
The glimmer of her rightful fate
is vanished soon as dew.

Her sullied skirts are torn and thorns
her errant steps confound
My Mother's heart the distance mourns
and sues to salve those wounds.

The Crook and Mitre blight her sight
Stiff doctrine is her yoke,
unbending where love lacks the might
celestial fire to stoke.

But I am coming through the mist
to meet her in the green
as nascent spring unfolds her bliss,
transports to lands unseen.

And now she's bonded to my heart,
My Bride, my Cherished Bride,
and she will never more depart
but in my breast abide.

Bread Of Heaven And Roses

'What you do speaks so loudly that I cannot hear what you say.'
Ralph Waldo Emerson

If Emerson had asked your mother
'Tell me what you know'
he would have missed her whisper
She could pluck, unpierced,
the thorny rose
disseminate its perfume,
discover no invisible worm,
She was loving living
and living loving
not buried in getting ready to live
She knew that the substance
of generous giving
was in asking for Grace
and baking the bread of sharing
with the leaven of trust,
humour and humility,
which cast on the waters
did that Galilee thing

and, as Cervantes noted,
helped to drown sorrow
Transcendent skies
weren't the bread of her eyes,
but the kindness kindling
warm light in a lonely eye,
a gleam and dream
of harmonies long-forgotten
yet just over the horizon
This, this was Panis Angelicus'
blessed morsels falling freely
under her ample table.

To peddle Emerson's lexicon
would have wasted litanies
She knew by instinct
that what lies behind
and what lies before
are tiny matters compared
to what lies within
She could not do a kindness
too soon, for she knew well enough
how soon it might be too late.

Your mother hitched her wagon

to her namesake's crown of stars,
her *'Yes!'* to life in every breath,
gesture and neatly sewn prayer,
proclaiming a destiny fulfilled
to the women at the gates,
her mortal shoes treading the earth
that weeps and laughs in flowers,
her inner child the while
inhabiting the courts of heaven.

Ruby Wedding

Incident on an ordinary Monday

Crimson rose called Ruby Wedding,
not a gift to me,
Jewelled rose, your bounty bleeding
blossom from the tree

Velvet bee that sweet heart singing,
trapped inside the glass,
on pane of death, its life-force squand'ring,
echoes of the Mass

Limpid wall of stings and sighing,
communion averse
God by woman's hand supplying
rescue from the curse

Wings upswept on morning gilded
home on smiling rose
In her silken petals folded,
bee his purpose knows

The Cello

The cello
etches its molten music
into the psyche

steals the soul
an aural apparition
passing through locked doors

string breezes
sing, burgeoning from chaos
resonance beckons

harmony
conjures vision timeless as
future memory

subsumed joy
Theia with shadows dancing
the light fantastic

cello truth
is baritone, the plumbed stave
sounds close melody

Epiphany

The caskets open,
Pandora's curse rescinded
Hope flies free to roost
under sullen earthly eaves,
entropy entombed.

Gold tells a Kingdom
whose secret interior
banishes despair,
mineral mined and refined
with yearning and faith.

Frankincense, sacred
sap, prayer's pleading perfume
hints Gethsemane,
salve of pain in mortal wounds,
the world ebbs away.

Myrrh for sacrifice,
sweet emollient from thorns
crowning Lamb of God,
chrism of sins turned to ash
Death subsumed in Life.

These prescient gifts
brought by bone-weary pilgrims,
followers of Light,
diviners of True Order,
tell what tongue cannot.

Breakthrough

The sky, a ceiling of sallow floc
compresses the breath, the mind, the will
all aspiration chained to foreground
a trudging evolution of sepic moments
jejune obsessions, tawdry distraction
the ether's trails filtered to murk
suggesting, to the unschooled eye,
a natural climatic malaise

No solar orientation
the map forgotten, destiny
opaque, a fading thought
Age of gold neither memory nor vision

Smokescreen and camouflage
can no more obscure the origin of life
than expiate the consequence of hubris
Behind the veil, above it and within,
breathes the vibrant prospect meant for us
Breeze hints, wind spins the theme, shrouds rag
Gulls soar through shimmering air

in a paradise of fourth dimensional blue...

It is still the Creator's world

Uriel's Token

'Flowers appear on the earth;
the season of singing has come,
the cooing of doves
is heard in our land.'
Song of Songs

To capture images
of a summer garden
is like culling fruit
to preserve and savour,
parade on the screen-shelf
fit for winter, when sap drains,
colour shrinks from truant sun
and the fulsome songs of birds
and fevered insects are muted

This once was
and will be again
an ever-amplified rebirth

Though sticks of winter

cringe in silent frost,
bones ache in cruel winds
that claw at heartbeats
but circumvent the frame
cocooned in quilting,
the Archangel of Summer
will one day appear
and reveal his abiding realm

www.ingramcontent.com/pod-product-compliance
Lightning Source LLC
Chambersburg PA
CBHW071307040426
42444CB00009B/1917